The Third Book of Baruch

A Visionary Journey Through Heaven and Earth

A Modern Translation

Adapted for the Contemporary Reader

Anonymous
(Jewish Historian)

Translated by Tim Zengerink

© **Copyright 2025**
All rights reserved.

It is not legal to reproduce, duplicate, or transmit any part of this document in either electronic means or in printed format. Recording of this publication is strictly prohibited and any storage of this document is not allowed unless with written permission from the publisher except for the use of brief quotations in a book review.

This book contains works of fiction. Any resemblance to persons living or dead, or places, events, or locations is purely coincidental.

Table Of Contents

Preface - Message to the Reader 1
Introduction 5
Chapter 1 14
Chapter II 16
Chapter III 18
Chapter IV 20
Chapter V 26
Chapter VI 27
Chapter VII 30
Chapter VIII 31
Chapter IX 33
Chapter X 35
Chapter XI 37
Chapter XII 39
Chapter XIII 41
Chapter XIV 43
Chapter XV 44
Chapter XVI 45
Chapter XVII 46
Thank You for Reading 47

Preface - Message to the Reader

What If You Could Help Rebuild the Greatest Library in Human History?

Thousands of years ago, the Library of Alexandria stood as the crown jewel of human achievement — a sanctuary where the collected wisdom of every known civilization was gathered, preserved, and shared freely.

And then, it was lost.

Through fire, conquest, and the slow erosion of time, humanity lost not just books — but ideas, dreams, discoveries, and stories that could have changed the world forever.

Today, the Library of Alexandria lives again — and you are invited to be a part of its restoration.

Our mission is simple yet profound:

To rebuild the greatest library the world has ever known, and to translate all timeless works into every language and dialect, so that no seeker of knowledge is ever left behind again.

By joining our movement to rebuild the modern Library of Alexandria, you become part of an unprecedented mission:

- **Unlimited Access to the Greatest Audiobooks & eBooks Ever Written:**

  Instantly explore thousands of legendary works—Plato, Shakespeare, Jane Austen, Leo Tolstoy, and countless more. All instantly available to read or listen, placing a complete literary universe at your fingertips.

- **Beautiful Paperback & Deluxe Editions at Printing Cost**

  Own any title as an elegant paperback, deluxe hardcover, or stunning collectible boxset—offered to you at true printing cost, delivered straight to your door. Build your personal Library of Alexandria, crafted for beauty, built for durability, and worthy of proud display.

- **Fresh Translations for Modern Readers—in Every Language & Dialect**

  Enjoy timeless masterpieces reimagined in clear, contemporary language—no more outdated phrases or obscure references. Alongside the original versions, we're tirelessly translating these classics into every language and dialect imaginable, ensuring accessibility and understanding across cultures and generations.

- **Join a Global Renaissance of Literature & Knowledge**

    You directly support expanding our library, publishing deluxe editions at true cost, translating works into all global languages, and bringing humanity's greatest stories to people everywhere. By joining today, you're not just preserving a legacy of masterpieces; you set in motion a powerful wave of literary accessibility.

Become a Torchbearer of Knowledge.

Join us for free now at **LibraryofAlexandria.com**

Together, we will ensure that the light of human wisdom never fades again.

With gratitude and a shared love of knowledge,

The Modern Library of Alexandria Team

Visit:

www.libraryofalexandria.com

Or scan the code below:

Introduction

The Third Book of Baruch is one of the most fascinating and obscure texts in the tradition of Jewish apocalyptic literature. For centuries, it has remained on the periphery of both religious scholarship and popular spiritual thought—largely hidden from mainstream readers, referenced in academic circles only in passing, and rarely presented in a form that invites contemplation from a modern audience. Yet, within its brief but profound narrative lies a spiritual vision that deserves to be revisited, not only for its historical and theological value but also for the deeply personal questions it raises about the nature of creation, judgment, righteousness, and humanity's place in the cosmos.

This new edition, The Third Book of Baruch: A Visionary Journey Through Heaven and Earth – A Modern Translation – Adapted for the Contemporary Reader, seeks to open this hidden treasure to the modern world. It offers more than just a translation—it is an invitation. An invitation to walk beside the prophet Baruch as he ascends through the celestial spheres, guided by an angelic being who reveals, step by step, the divine architecture of heaven and the secrets that govern both the visible and invisible worlds.

But before you begin your journey through this mysterious and powerful text, it is worth preparing yourself for what you are about to encounter. The ancient writers of apocalyptic visions did not craft their messages lightly. These texts were often written in times of persecution, loss, or cultural crisis. They are not casual narratives but deeply symbolic and spiritually charged responses to the suffering of the world and the silence of heaven. The questions these works wrestle with are not abstract—they are visceral. Why do the wicked prosper? What happens after death? Is there justice beyond what we can see? And if so, who governs it?

To understand The Third Book of Baruch, we must begin by situating it within the broader world of apocalyptic thought and Jewish mysticism, then delve into the structure of the vision itself, its themes, symbols, and spiritual insights. Along the way, we'll uncover its connection to other ancient texts—especially the Book of Enoch, 2 Baruch, and other pseudepigraphical writings—and explore how this short yet powerful journey through the heavens continues to speak to us today.

The Apocalyptic Tradition

The genre of apocalypse is often misunderstood. Today, the word "apocalypse" conjures images of destruction, chaos, and end-times judgment. But in its original Greek, apokalypsis simply means "unveiling" or "revelation." In ancient Jewish and early Christian writings, apocalyptic literature was concerned not only with the end of the world but with the hidden truths that lay beyond ordinary perception—truths about divine justice, cosmic order, and the ultimate destiny of humanity.

These writings typically take the form of visionary journeys, in which a prophet or sage is led by a heavenly guide through a series of spiritual realms. Along the way, they receive revelations about the nature of sin and righteousness, the fate of the soul, and the workings of divine judgment. These journeys serve both to affirm the faith of the righteous and to challenge the complacency of the wicked. They are visionary in the truest sense—literature meant not only to inform but to transform the reader.

The Third Book of Baruch falls squarely within this tradition. It is a text that reveals what is hidden: the invisible workings of heaven, the spiritual architecture of the cosmos, and the moral structure upon which divine judgment is based. Though it is much shorter than many of its apocalyptic counterparts, it is no less profound.

Baruch: The Visionary and Scribe

The character of Baruch is well known in Jewish and Christian pseudepigrapha. Traditionally identified as the scribe and companion of the prophet Jeremiah, Baruch is associated with wisdom, mourning, and prophetic insight. In 2 Baruch, also known as The Apocalypse of Baruch, he laments the destruction of Jerusalem and seeks answers from God about the suffering of his people. In 3 Baruch, his role continues as that of a seeker—one who dares to ask the most difficult questions and who is granted a vision of divine reality as a response.

It's important to note that The Third Book of Baruch is not considered canonical in Judaism or most Christian traditions, though it appears in some versions of the Eastern Orthodox tradition. Its very existence, however, testifies to the spiritual hunger of the communities that preserved it. In a time when the world seemed broken, and the heavens silent, this book offered a glimpse beyond the veil—a reassurance that divine justice still operated, even if unseen.

Structure of the Vision

The structure of The Third Book of Baruch is deceptively simple. The text is framed as a visionary ascent through five heavens, each revealing a new level of divine operation and moral insight. At each level, Baruch witnesses strange and awe-inspiring scenes: an eagle guarding the entrance to heaven, a dragon being punished for transgressing divine boundaries, and various celestial beings tasked with administering aspects of creation and justice.

These visions are often presented in cryptic, symbolic language, with brief explanatory dialogues between Baruch and his angelic guide. While modern readers may be tempted to decode these symbols into rigid theological formulas, it is better to approach them with the eyes of a mystic than those of a systematizer. The visions are not meant to be puzzles to be solved, but revelations to be contemplated. Like a dream, their power lies in their capacity to resonate, to disturb, to enlighten—not merely to explain.

Key Themes and Teachings

Several key themes run throughout The Third Book of Baruch, forming a spiritual tapestry that is both cosmic and deeply personal.

1. Divine Order and Cosmic Justice

The entire structure of the heavens, as revealed to Baruch, operates on principles of justice, balance, and divine intention. Nothing is random. Each level of creation serves a purpose, and each being—whether angelic or beastly—is judged according to its deeds. This is a central message of the book: God's justice is real, even if hidden from earthly eyes.

2. Sin, Punishment, and the Role of the Celestial Beings

Throughout the text, Baruch witnesses beings who are punished for stepping outside the bounds of their divine mandate. Whether it is a dragon who transgresses its domain, or humans who rebel against the moral order, the consequence is clear: divine judgment is inevitable. Yet even in punishment, there is a sense of order—not chaos. Justice is not vengeance; it is correction and restoration.

3. The Ascent of the Righteous

The very act of Baruch's ascent is symbolic. It mirrors the spiritual journey of the soul—from confusion and sorrow to enlightenment and understanding. Each level of heaven represents a higher state of awareness, a clearer perception of divine truth. Baruch's questions—and the answers he receives—model the soul's own search for meaning.

4. Mystery and Revelation

This book is soaked in mystery. The heavens are strange, the creatures otherworldly, the logic often nonlinear. But this is not a flaw—it is the nature of true revelation. Apocalyptic literature does not flatten reality; it expands it. It does not offer easy answers but invites the reader into deeper and deeper reflection.

Connection to Jewish Mysticism

Though not a Kabbalistic text per se, The Third Book of Baruch is deeply mystical in its worldview. The layered heavens, the mediation of angelic beings, the emphasis on divine names and functions—all echo later Jewish mystical traditions. The vision of the cosmos as a living, ordered system governed by spiritual laws is central to both early apocalyptic texts and later mystical thought.

In this sense, reading 3 Baruch is not merely an exercise in ancient literature—it is a spiritual practice. It trains the imagination to think cosmically, to see life as part of a vast and holy mystery, to recognize that the divine is present even when hidden.

Translated by Tim Zengerink

Why This Modern Translation?

Many existing translations of The Third Book of Baruch are either overly academic or outdated in language, making the text feel distant and difficult to engage with. This modern translation was crafted with a specific goal: to preserve the visionary power and symbolic depth of the original while making it fully accessible to contemporary readers.

The text has been translated sentence by sentence, retaining the structure, flow, and symbolism without reducing or simplifying its content. Archaic phrases have been replaced with clear, natural language, but never at the cost of spiritual meaning. The aim is not to demystify the text—but to open the door wider, so that readers today can enter its mysteries with clarity and awe.

How to Read This Book

To get the most out of The Third Book of Baruch, approach it as you would a sacred journey. This is not a book to be rushed through but one to sit with. Read each chapter slowly. Pause after each vision. Reflect on the symbols, the dialogue, the questions raised. If you find yourself confused, that is part of the process. The text was designed to stir the soul more than satisfy the mind.

You may wish to keep a journal of your reflections as you read. What emotions arise in you as Baruch ascends each heaven? Which images linger in your mind? What spiritual insights do you draw from the scenes of judgment and restoration?

Final Thoughts

In a time of uncertainty, injustice, and spiritual longing, The Third Book of Baruch offers a vision of hope rooted in divine order. It reminds us that the universe is not random, that justice is real even when delayed, and that those who seek truth with humility and courage will be guided—even through the heavens themselves.

Whether you are a student of ancient texts, a seeker of mystical wisdom, or simply a curious reader yearning for insight, this book has something to offer you. It is short in length but vast in implication.

As you turn the page and begin your own ascent with Baruch, may you find not only answers, but also the questions that matter most. May you discover, hidden in its strange and luminous pages, the same wisdom that has inspired mystics and visionaries for generations.

Welcome to The Third Book of Baruch. The journey begins now.

Chapter 1

I, Baruch, was deeply troubled and filled with sorrow as I thought about the suffering of my people. My heart ached, and I mourned over how King Nebuchadnezzar had been allowed by the Almighty to destroy the holy city. I struggled to understand why this had happened to us. Crying out, I said, "Lord, why did you allow your vineyard to be ruined? Why have you let it be destroyed? Why did you punish us in this way instead of disciplining us differently? Instead, you handed us over to these nations that now mock us, saying, 'Where is their God?'"

As these thoughts overwhelmed me, tears streamed down my face, and my heart grew heavier with sorrow. But as I wept, pouring out my grief, a vision appeared before me. I saw an angel of the Lord descending with a bright and powerful presence. He came near and spoke to me, saying, "Man of God, greatly loved, do not let your heart be so burdened over the fate of Jerusalem. Listen to the words of the Almighty, for He has sent me to reveal His divine plan to you."

The angel continued, "This is what the Lord God Almighty says: Your prayer has been heard, Baruch. The Most High has received your cries and your sorrow. He has seen the pain in your heart and has listened to your words."

Hearing this, I began to feel a sense of calm, though my mind was still filled with questions. The angel, sensing my uncertainty, said, "Do not trouble yourself by trying to understand everything right now. The ways of God are beyond what you can see. I have been sent to show you things far greater than what you have asked. These are truths beyond your understanding at this moment."

With deep respect, I replied, "As surely as the Lord lives, I will not question or complain if you reveal these mysteries to me. And if I fail to keep this promise, may God judge me on the day of reckoning."

Then the angel, speaking with both authority and kindness, said, "Come, Baruch. Follow me, and I will show you the hidden and sacred things of the Most High. Open your heart to receive these truths, for they will bring light to your soul and wisdom to your spirit."

At that moment, I resolved to listen, ready to receive the knowledge that the Lord was about to reveal through His messenger. My sorrow began to change into anticipation as I followed the angel, preparing to understand the deep and eternal wisdom of the Almighty.

Chapter II

The angel took me with him to where the heavens were firmly set in place. There, I saw an enormous river—so wide that no one could cross it, not even the foreign nations that God had created. Then, he led me further and took me up to the first heaven, where we arrived at a massive door. He turned to me and said, "Let's go inside."

As we entered, it felt as if we were flying, traveling a distance that would have taken thirty days to walk.

Inside, I saw a vast plain stretching across the heaven. There were beings living there, but they looked different from humans. Their faces resembled cattle, they had horns like deer, feet like goats, and their lower bodies were covered in wool like sheep.

I, Baruch, turned to the angel and asked, "Please tell me, how thick is this heaven we passed through? How wide is it? And what is this plain you have shown me? I want to share this with the people on earth."

The angel, whose name was Phamael, answered, "The door you saw is the gateway to heaven. Its thickness is as great as the distance from earth to heaven, and the width of the plain you saw is just as vast."

Then the angel said, "Come with me, and I will show you even greater mysteries."

I asked him, "Please tell me, who are these people?"

He replied, "They are the ones who built the great tower, trying to fight against God. Because of their actions, the Lord removed them from the earth."

Chapter III

The angel of the Lord took me up to the second heaven and showed me a door that looked just like the first one. He said, "Let's go inside." So we entered, traveling as if we were flying, covering a distance that would take sixty days to walk.

Inside, I saw another vast plain, and it was filled with people. But their appearance was strange—they had faces like dogs and feet like deer.

I asked the angel, "Who are these people?"

He answered, "These are the ones who planned to build the great tower. They forced many men and women to make bricks for the construction. Among them was a woman who was forced to keep working even while she was giving birth. They did not allow her to stop, so she gave birth while making bricks. She wrapped her baby in her cloak and continued working.

When the Lord appeared to them, He confused their languages. By that time, they had already built the tower up to a height of 463 cubits. Then they took a tool and tried to drill through the sky, saying, 'Let's see if heaven is made of clay, copper, or iron.'

When God saw what they were doing, He did not let them continue. Instead, He struck them with blindness and caused their speech to become confused. That is why they are as you see them now."

Chapter IV

I, Baruch, said, "Lord, you have already shown me incredible and amazing things. Now, I ask you, for the Lord's sake, to show me everything else."

The angel replied, "Come, let's go further." We traveled together, covering a distance that would take about 185 days to walk.

He led me to a vast plain where I saw a massive serpent that looked like it was made of stone. Then, he showed me Hades, a place that was dark, empty, and unclean.

I asked, "What is this dragon, and what is the creature surrounding it?"

The angel explained, "This dragon devours the bodies of those who lived wicked lives. It feeds on them. Hades works the same way—it consumes and never stops. Each day, it takes about a cubit of water from the sea, yet the sea never runs dry."

I asked, "How is that possible?"

The angel said, "Listen carefully. The Lord created 360 rivers, and the three largest ones are the Alphias, the Aburos, and the Gerikos. These rivers constantly flow into the sea, keeping it from ever running out."

Then I said, "Please show me the tree that caused Adam to go astray."

The angel answered, "That tree is actually a vine, planted by the angel Samail. It made the Lord angry, and He cursed both Samail and the vine. That's why God commanded Adam not to touch it. The devil, out of jealousy, used it to deceive Adam."

I asked, "If the vine was so dangerous and brought a curse upon Adam, why does it still serve an important purpose today?"

The angel replied, "That is a good question. When God sent the flood to destroy all living things, including 409,000 giants, the water rose 15 cubits above the highest mountains. The flood reached Paradise and wiped out every plant and flower. However, a small branch of the vine was carried by the waters and left on the earth.

"When the flood ended and the land appeared again, Noah came out of the ark and began planting everything he found. Among them, he discovered the vine branch. He wasn't sure what it was and prayed for guidance. That's when I came to him and explained its origin.

"Noah asked, 'Should I plant this, or should I destroy it? Since Adam was cursed because of it, will I also bring God's anger upon myself if I plant it?' He was unsure, so he prayed for forty days, pleading with God to tell him what to do.

"Finally, God sent the angel Sarasel with a message. The angel told Noah, 'Plant the vine. The Lord says this: What was once bitter will become sweet, what was cursed will become a blessing, and its fruit will represent the blood of God. Just as humanity was condemned through it, through Jesus Christ, Emmanuel, it will now offer a way back into Paradise.'

"Remember this, Baruch: Just as Adam was cursed and lost God's glory because of this vine, people today also fall further from God when they drink too much wine. By overindulging, they bring judgment upon themselves and prepare for eternal punishment.

"Nothing good comes from drinking in excess. Those who drink too much commit terrible sins: brothers turn against brothers, fathers lose compassion for their sons, children stop respecting their parents, and because of drunkenness, all kinds of evil arise—murder, adultery, immorality, lying, stealing, and many other sins. Truly, no good comes from it."

I, Baruch, said, "Lord, you have already shown me amazing and powerful things. Now, I ask you, for the sake of the Lord, to show me everything else."

The angel replied, "Come, let's go further." We traveled together, covering a distance that would take about 185 days to walk.

He led me to a vast plain where I saw a huge serpent that looked as if it were made of stone. Then, he showed me Hades—a dark, empty, and unclean place.

I asked, "What is this dragon, and what is the creature surrounding it?"

The angel explained, "This dragon feeds on the bodies of those who lived sinful lives. It grows stronger by consuming them. Hades works the same way—it takes from the world, but never runs out. Every day, it absorbs a cubit of water from the sea, yet the sea never shrinks."

I asked, "How is that possible?"

The angel said, "Listen carefully. The Lord created 360 rivers, and the three largest ones are the Alphias, the Aburos, and the Gerikos. These rivers flow constantly into the sea, keeping it from ever running dry."

Then I said, "Please show me the tree that led Adam astray."

The angel answered, "That tree is actually a vine, planted by the angel Samail. It angered the Lord, and

He cursed both Samail and the vine. That is why God commanded Adam not to touch it. The devil, out of jealousy, used it to deceive Adam."

I asked, "If this vine caused such harm and was cursed by God, why does it still have such an important purpose?"

The angel replied, "That is a good question. When God sent the great flood to destroy all living things, including 409,000 giants, the water rose 15 cubits above the highest mountains. The flood even reached Paradise, wiping out every plant and flower. However, a small branch of the vine was carried by the waters and left on the earth.

"When the flood ended and the land reappeared, Noah left the ark and began planting the things he found. Among them, he discovered the vine branch. He was unsure what it was and prayed for guidance. That's when I came to him and explained its origin.

"Noah asked, 'Should I plant this, or should I destroy it? Since Adam was cursed because of it, will I also bring God's anger upon myself if I plant it?' He was uncertain, so he prayed for forty days, asking God to tell him what to do.

"Finally, God sent the angel Sarasel with a message. The angel told Noah, 'Plant the vine. The Lord says this: What was once bitter will become sweet, what was cursed will become a blessing, and its fruit will represent the blood of God. Just as humanity was condemned through it, through Jesus Christ, Emmanuel, it will now offer a way back into Paradise.'

"Remember this, Baruch: Just as Adam was cursed and lost God's glory because of this vine, people today also fall further from God when they drink too much wine. By overindulging, they bring judgment upon themselves and prepare for eternal punishment.

"Nothing good comes from drinking excessively. Those who do become reckless and commit terrible sins: brothers turn against brothers, fathers lose compassion for their children, children stop respecting their parents, and because of drunkenness, all kinds of evil arise—murder, adultery, immorality, lying, stealing, and many other wrongs. Truly, nothing good comes from it."

Chapter V

I, Baruch, turned to the angel and asked, "Lord, may I ask you something?"

The angel replied, "Ask whatever you wish."

I continued, "You told me that the serpent drinks a cubit of water from the sea each day. Can you tell me how big its stomach is?"

The angel answered, "Its stomach is as large as Hades itself. It is so massive that it stretches as far as a group of 300 men could throw a heavy stone."

Then he said, "Come with me, and I will show you things even greater than this."

Chapter VI

The angel took me to the place where the sun rises.

He showed me a chariot pulled by four horses, with fire blazing beneath it. A man sat on the chariot, wearing a crown made of flames. Around the chariot stood forty angels, and in front of it ran a massive bird—so large that it looked as big as nine mountains.

I asked the angel, "What is this bird?"

He answered, "This is the guardian of the world."

I asked again, "How does this bird protect the world? Please explain it to me."

The angel said, "This bird travels with the sun as it moves. It spreads its wings to absorb the sun's fiery rays. If it didn't do this, the heat would be too strong, and no living creature—human or animal—would survive. That is why God created this bird for this purpose."

Then the bird spread its wings, and I saw large letters written on its right wing. The letters covered a huge space, about the size of a threshing floor, around 4,000 measures wide. They shined like gold.

The angel said, "Read what is written."

So I read the letters, and they said: "Neither the earth nor the heavens can hold me, but the wings of fire carry me."

I asked the angel, "What is the name of this bird?"

He replied, "It is called the Phoenix."

I asked, "What does it eat?"

He answered, "It feeds on manna from heaven and the dew of the earth."

I asked again, "Does it produce waste?"

The angel replied, "Yes, it excretes a worm, and from this, cinnamon is formed. This cinnamon is used by kings and rulers. But wait, and you will see the glory of God."

While the angel was still speaking, a sudden thunderclap shook the ground beneath us.

I asked, "What is this sound?"

The angel explained, "The angels are opening the 365 gates of heaven, allowing light to separate from darkness."

Then I heard a voice say, "Light-giver, bring splendor to the world!"

At that moment, I also heard the bird's call and asked, "What is that sound?"

The angel answered, "This is the cry that wakes the roosters on earth. Just as people signal each other, the rooster announces the start of the day. As the angels prepare the sun, the rooster crows to let the earth know morning has come."

Chapter VII

I asked, "Where does the sun begin its journey after the rooster crows?"

The angel replied, "Listen, Baruch, everything I have shown you so far is within the first and second heavens. But in the third heaven, the sun moves through and spreads its light across the world. Be patient, and you will see the glory of God."

As the angel spoke, I saw the bird appear again. At first, it looked small, but it grew larger and larger until it returned to its full size.

Following the bird, I saw the sun shining brightly, surrounded by angels who carried it. A magnificent crown rested on the sun, and its light was so intense that we couldn't look directly at it.

At the same moment, the phoenix spread its wings wide. The brilliance of the scene was overwhelming, and I was filled with such fear that I turned away and hid under the angel's wings.

The angel reassured me, saying, "Do not be afraid, Baruch. Stay here, and soon you will see the sun as it sets."

Chapter VIII

He led me toward the west, and as the sun neared the horizon, I once again saw the great bird flying ahead, guiding the sun. The sun followed closely behind, surrounded by angels. When it reached its resting place, I watched as the angels removed the crown from its head. The bird, exhausted from its journey, let its wings droop as if weighed down by fatigue.

Curious about what I had seen, I asked, "Why do the angels take the crown off the sun's head? And why does the bird look so tired?"

The angel explained, "At the end of each day, four angels carry the sun's crown to heaven so that it can be renewed. This is necessary because, as the sun travels over the earth, its rays and crown become tainted. Each day, they must be cleansed and restored."

I then asked, "How do the sun's rays become unclean?"

The angel replied, "As the sun shines on the earth, it witnesses the sins of humanity. These include acts of immorality, stealing, violence, idolatry, drunkenness, murder, jealousy, gossip, deceit, and many other things that offend God. Because of this, the sun's light becomes stained and must be purified daily."

Wanting to understand more, I asked, "Why is the bird so worn out?"

The angel answered, "The bird is exhausted because it spends the entire day protecting the earth from the full heat of the sun. It spreads its wings to absorb the intense rays so that they don't burn everything below. Without its constant effort, as I told you before, no living thing would be able to survive the sun's scorching heat."

Chapter IX

When night arrived, the moon and stars appeared in the sky. I, Baruch, turned to the angel and asked, "Lord, please explain this to me as well. Where does the moon go when it disappears, and what path does it follow?"

The angel replied, "Be patient, and soon you will see and understand."

The next day, I saw the moon. It looked like a woman seated in a chariot with wheels. In front of the chariot were oxen and lambs, and many angels traveled alongside it.

I asked, "Lord, what are the oxen and lambs?"

The angel answered, "These are also angels."

I then asked, "Why does the moon sometimes appear larger and at other times smaller?"

The angel explained, "Listen, Baruch. The moon was created by God to be beautiful and unique. However, during Adam's first sin, the moon gave its light to Samael when he took the form of the serpent. Instead of hiding its brightness, it shined even more. This angered God, so He reduced its light and shortened its days."

I asked, "Why doesn't the moon shine all the time, but only at night?"

The angel replied, "Just as servants do not speak freely in the presence of a king, the moon and stars cannot shine in the presence of the sun. The stars remain in their places, but their light is overpowered by the sun's brightness. Meanwhile, the moon is safe, but its light fades because of the sun's intense heat and brilliance."

Chapter X

After the archangel had taught me all these things, he led me to the third heaven. There, I saw a vast, endless plain, and in the center was a peaceful lake of clear water. Surrounding the lake were many birds of all kinds, but they were unlike any birds I had ever seen on earth. Among them, I noticed a crane as large as an ox. All of the birds were magnificent, far greater than anything found in the world below.

I turned to the angel and asked, "What is this plain? What is this lake? And why are so many birds gathered around it?"

The angel replied, "Listen carefully, Baruch. This plain, which holds many hidden mysteries, is where the souls of the righteous come together. Here, they live in peace and form choirs to praise the Lord."

He continued, "The water in this lake is what the clouds draw up to bring rain to the earth. That rain helps plants grow and produce fruit."

I then asked, "And what about these birds?"

The angel answered, "These birds never stop singing praises to the Lord."

I, Baruch, then said, "Lord, why do people say that rain comes from the sea?"

The angel explained, "Some rain does come from the sea and from water sources on the earth. But the rain that helps crops grow comes from this place. From now on, understand that what people call the 'dew of heaven' also comes from here."

Chapter XI

The angel led me from that place to the fifth heaven. When we arrived, I saw that the gate was closed. I asked, "Lord, will the gate be opened so we can enter?"

The angel replied, "We cannot go in until Michael, the one who holds the keys to heaven, arrives. Be patient, and you will see the glory of God."

Suddenly, a loud noise like thunder filled the air. I asked, "Lord, what is that sound?"

The angel answered, "It is the archangel Michael descending to collect the prayers of people on earth."

Then a voice called out, "Let the gate be opened!" At that moment, the gate swung open with a sound as powerful as a thunderclap.

Michael appeared, and the angel with me stepped forward, bowing low and saying, "Greetings, commander of all the heavenly armies."

Michael replied, "Greetings to you as well, our brother and messenger of God's revelations to the righteous."

After they exchanged greetings, they stood together. Then, I saw Michael holding a massive bowl. It was so large that its depth stretched from heaven to earth, and its width reached from north to south.

Amazed, I asked, "Lord, what is that bowl that the archangel Michael is carrying?"

The angel answered, "This bowl holds the virtues and good deeds of the righteous. Michael gathers them and presents them before God in heaven."

Chapter XII

As I was speaking with them, I saw angels approaching, each carrying baskets filled with beautiful flowers. They brought these baskets to Michael and handed them over. Curious, I turned to the angel beside me and asked, "Lord, who are these angels, and what are they carrying?"

He answered, "These are the angels responsible for overseeing different regions and nations."

I watched as Michael took the baskets from the angels and emptied the flowers into the large bowl he was holding. Then, the angel explained, "The flowers being poured into the bowl represent the good deeds and virtues of the righteous."

As I looked closer, I noticed other angels arriving, but their baskets were not completely full. These angels seemed troubled and hesitant, standing back instead of stepping forward. It was clear they hadn't gathered enough to fill their baskets.

Michael saw their hesitation and called out, "Come forward, you angels, and bring whatever you have collected."

Translated by Tim Zengerink

They obeyed, but as they poured what little they had into the bowl, both Michael and the angel beside me looked deeply saddened. The contributions from these angels were not enough to fill the bowl completely.

Chapter XIII

Then, more angels arrived, crying and trembling with fear. They said, "Look at us, Lord! We have become stained and darkened because we were assigned to serve evil people. Please, we beg you, remove us from their presence."

Michael replied, "You cannot leave them, for we must not let the enemy claim victory. But tell me, what do you wish?"

The angels answered, ** "Michael, our commander, we ask you to take us away from them. We can no longer bear being among these wicked and corrupt people. They have no goodness in them—only greed and wrongdoing.

"We have never seen them enter a place of worship, seek guidance from spiritual leaders, or do anything righteous. Instead, wherever there is murder, they are involved. Wherever there is immorality, theft, lies, jealousy, drunkenness, violence, or idolatry, they are at the center of it all. Their actions are evil, and they continue in their wickedness without regret. Please, release us from them.

Translated by Tim Zengerink

Michael turned to them and said, "Wait here while I seek the Lord's will to find out what should be done."

Chapter XIV

At that moment, Michael left, and the large doors closed tightly behind him. A deep, powerful sound, like rolling thunder, echoed through the heavens.

I turned to the angel beside me and asked, "What is that loud noise?"

The angel replied, "That is Michael presenting the good deeds of people before God."

Chapter XV

At that moment, Michael returned, and the gate opened. He carried oil with him.

For the angels who had brought full baskets, he filled them with oil and said, "Take this and give a hundredfold reward to our friends—those who have worked hard and done good. Those who have planted well will harvest well."

To the angels who had brought half-filled baskets, he said, "Come and receive your reward based on what you brought, and deliver it to the people on earth."

Then, speaking to both groups—the ones with full baskets and those with half-filled ones—he said, "Go and bless our friends. Tell them that the Lord says: 'You have been faithful with little, so I will give you even more. Enter into the joy of the Lord.'"

Chapter XVI

Then he turned to those who had brought nothing and said, **"Do not be sad, and do not weep, but do not abandon the people on earth either.

Since they have angered me with their actions, go and make them jealous. Stir their frustration and turn their hearts against those who are not even a nation, against people who lack understanding.

Send swarms of caterpillars and locusts, rust and grasshoppers. Strike them with hail, lightning, and fury. Bring punishment through the sword and death, and send demons to trouble their children.

For they refused to listen to my voice. They ignored my commands and did not follow them. Instead, they rejected my instructions, turned away from my places of worship, and insulted the priests who spoke my words to them.

Chapter XVII

As he finished speaking, the door closed, **and we stepped away.

The angel then led me back to the place where my journey had first begun.

When I came to my senses, I praised God for allowing me to witness such incredible things.

And to you, my brothers who read these revelations, give glory to God, so that He may also honor us—now and forever, for all eternity! Amen.

Thank You for Reading

Dear Reader,

We hope this timeless classic has sparked your imagination and enriched your literary journey. Now that you've turned the final page, we want to share a vision for the future of reading—one where every classic you've ever wanted to explore is at your fingertips, in a format that best suits your life.

We'd like to invite you to gain immediate, unlimited digital & audiobook access to hundreds of the most treasured literary classics ever written—along with the option to secure deluxe paperback, hardcover & box set editions at printing cost. Together, we can spark a new global literary renaissance alongside our small, independent publishing house called "The Library of Alexandria."

Thousands of years ago, the Library of Alexandria stood as a beacon of knowledge—until it was lost to history. We aim to reignite that spirit of preservation and discovery right now, in the modern age—only this time, it's accessible to all, in every language and every format.

Picture a world where every timeless classic, novel, poem, or philosophical treatise is not only available to read but also updated for today's readers—modernized, translated into any language or dialect, and ready to enjoy in any format you choose, whether that is in an eBook, audiobook, paperback, or deluxe hardcover & box set version a printing cost.

By joining our movement to rebuild the modern Library of Alexandria, you become part of an unprecedented mission to offer:

- **Unlimited Audiobook & eBook Access to the Greatest Classics of All Time**

    Instantly explore thousands of legendary works, from Plato and Shakespeare to Jane Austen and Leo Tolstoy. All are instantly ready to read or listen to, giving you a complete literary universe at your fingertips.

- **Paperback & Deluxe Editions at Printing Costs:**

    Purchase any title in a paperback, deluxe hardbound, or deluxe boxset edition at printing costs, shipped right to your doorstep. Curate your personal library of Alexandria with editions worthy of display—crafted to last, designed to captivate, and delivered straight to your door.

- **Modern translations for Contemporary Readers in all languages and dialects**

  Discover a vast selection of classics reimagined in clear, current language—no more struggling with outdated phrases or obscure references. Next to the original versions, we aim to offer translations in as many languages and dialects as possible.

  As we continue our translation efforts and add new languages, readers everywhere can connect with these works as if they were written today. By bridging linguistic divides, you're contributing to ensuring that these timeless stories become more meaningful, accessible, and inspiring for people across the globe.

- **Your Personal Library of Alexandria:**

  Over the months and years, you'll curate a unique physical archive of classics—each volume a testament to your taste, curiosity, and love of knowledge. It's not just about owning books—it's about curating a cultural legacy you'll cherish and pass down for generations to come.

- **Join a Global Literary Renaissance:**

  Your support fuels an ongoing mission: allowing us to reinvest in offering deluxe print editions (including special boxsets) at their true cost, broaden the range of available formats and translations, and extend the reach of these works to new audiences worldwide. By joining today, you're not just preserving a legacy of masterpieces; you set in motion a powerful wave of literary accessibility.

We are more than a publisher—we're a movement, and we can't do it alone. Your support lets us scale our mission, preserving and reimagining history's greatest works for tomorrow's readers.

Become a Torchbearer of knowledge.

Thank you for picking up this book and allowing us into your literary journey. As you turn the pages, know that you're part of something larger: a global effort to keep these stories alive, share their wisdom across borders and generations, and spark a true cultural revival for the modern era.

If this resonates with you—please consider taking the next step by visiting:

www.libraryofalexandria.com

With gratitude and a shared love of knowledge,

The Modern Library of Alexandria Team

Visit:

www.libraryofalexandria.com

Or scan the code below:

www.ingramcontent.com/pod-product-compliance
Lightning Source LLC
LaVergne TN
LVHW030631080426
835512LV00021B/3459